2213

Longing
for Intimacy
Glimmers of Hope

Prayers and Poems for Shining Light on Life's Mystery

Catherine L. Coates

FLOWER *of* LIFE PRESS

KUDOS

"Wow! It is truly astounding! There is such an outpouring of Grace, Hope, Devotion, and Love with the turn of each page. It's clear that she is not just putting pretty words on a page, but persevering the turbulence of life with something greater that flows like a river throughout the book, throughout her life. It is an inspired work of Love, born out of her resilience, tenacity and devotion to Holy Mystery and respect for what has been gifted to her as life."

—Don DeMercurio, Integral Life Path Counselor and Spiritual Healer

"Catherine Coates beautifully lays her heart bare in this brave and thoughtful collection that illuminates the journey through depression and offers hope at the same time. The work of finding and keeping faith will resonate with those struggling with adversity or questioning their beliefs. Coates' resilience is inspiring."

—Suzanne Washburn

"What Catherine has pulled together is an entirely honest and raw set of poetic ponderings. If you read these poems slowly enough, you begin to sense the depth of inquiry they are opening to, and it becomes clear that this isn't just about Catherine's journey. These poems are bread crumbs, leading us toward transcending but including our past. This is a journey toward wholeness."

—Nathan Brisby SHRM-SCP/MBA/MA/GC-C/PGRS-C/CMMT

"This book is a treasure trove of wisdom and love. I just finished it and am going to start again. Your writing is exquisite encompassing every aspect of feelings, life cycles, spiritual pearls of wisdom and most of all hope. It was an honor to read it and I can't wait for it to be available. It will help and inspire so many people."

—Rev. Sandy Fischman

"Too often, modern spiritual writing points to a self-affirming positivity which ignores the difficulties of walking a surrendered spiritual path. Luckily, in these intimate pages Catherine Coates has dared to show a less naïve experience, giving impassioned voice to the shadows which accompany any encounter with light. We are the better for her wise and intelligent companionship. Throughout these brave and honest meditations, Catherine shares the struggles of her own dark night: the soulful experience of despair and heartbreak which appear when our best efforts to find and connect to the divine are left unanswered. She offers gorgeous prayers along the way. From the lived experience of her own depression and painful struggles—and her steadfast longing and devotion—we are left with a true blessing of Mystery; that we may each live in the fullness of a compassionate, open, and accepting life, as a 'portal of wisdom' with humility. One such prayer from this collection includes this plea: 'Holy Spirit/May I be a channel of your/Presence this day./A lantern through which Your/Light shines. Throughout *Longing for Intimacy*, Catherine is such a shining lantern."

—REV. DAVID WALLACE, DEAN AND SENIOR TEACHER (RETIRED)
ONE SPIRIT INTERFAITH SEMINARY, NYC

"With utmost vulnerability and unceasing strength, Catherine Coates offers readers vivid snapshots of the sacred mess we call life. Through thought-provoking poems and useful prayers, she urges us to deepen our connection to that which is holy for us individually, and encourages us to jettison that which we've outgrown."

—SARAH A. BOWEN, AUTHOR OF *SPIRITUAL REBEL: A POSITIVELY ADDICTIVE GUIDE TO FINDING DEEPER PERSPECTIVE* AND *HIGHER PURPOSE*, DEAN AT ONE SPIRIT INTERFAITH SEMINARY

"Catherine Coates has really poured her heart and soul into this book."

—JUDY BRISTOW

FLOWER *of* LIFE PRESS

Longing For Intimacy—Glimmers of Hope:
Prayers and Poems for Shining Light on Life's Mystery
By Catherine L. Coates

Published by Flower of Life Press
Hadlyme, CT 06439

To contact the publisher, visit floweroflifepress.com

Book design by Astara Jane Ashley, floweroflifepress.com

Library of Congress Control Number: Available upon request

ISBN-13: 979-8-9873954-8-6

Printed in the United States of America

These pages are dedicated to my family: Steve and Carys, and our pomapoos, Sami who is no longer with us, and Gala who joins me at bedtime each night. Their love sustained me through the tough times, [and continues to support me today.]

In addition, I honor Don DeMercurio, who has been my life coach for over twenty years. His love and wisdom have guided me through the murky paths I have traveled.

And to Holy Mystery, with whom I have played hide and seek my whole life.

CONTENTS

PREFACE

Gentles:

These prayers and poems express my search for god, whom I call Holy Mystery. They are also an attempt to shine light on my struggle with depression. Mixed in are observations and attempts to make sense of life. Some of it isn't pretty. Depression isn't pretty. Very few answers are offered. One could almost read it as a memoir—a pouring out of my heart to shine light on my story.

One thing that might be surprising is my use of lower case for god. I do this when I am talking about something that doesn't reflect my concept of a god. (However, when I am quoting the New Revised Standard Version Updated Edition, I use the case from the text as is required by their copyright stipulations). My use of Latin, Greek, and Hebrew is a bit more obscure. All I can say is these languages came to me as I wrote. I think it functions to emphasize the mystery of the topics.

You'll also find a lot of references to the Bible, primarily the Psalms. These words are part of my heritage, and are rooted deeply in my soul. They spring to my mind as a natural part of my thought process.

These are my hopes for you as you peruse this volume. May you find an outlet for your grief and pain. And may you find glimmers of hope that there is Holy Mystery who loves you beyond measure. May you laugh and cry; sorrow and rejoice. Because the light at the end of the tunnel is not an on-coming train, rather it is the glow of hope.

Thank you for joining me on this journey toward wholeness.

~Catherine

ACKNOWLEDGMENTS

I started writing prayers in earnest after taking a seminar at One Spirit Learning Alliance. Nura Hirmina offered a study in writing prayers like the poets. This effort is, in part, the result of studying with her.

Helpers along my way included: John Karl, Beth Struever, Pat Youngdahl, Ellen Wondra, John Teleska, Stephen Benjamin, Rob Bauer, Robin Lane, Don DeMercurio, and the community at One Spirit Learning Alliance. In addition, this book would not exist without the loving direction from Astara, publisher of Flower of Life Press, and the Divine Writing Journey program.

Thank you to my readers: Sarah Bowen, Nathan Brisby, Judy Bristow, Sandy Fischman, Kathleen Keenan-Palumbos, Don DeMercurio, David Wallace, and Suzanne Washburn. Their supportive reflections have given me courage to move forward with this project.

You Are Loved

You are loved
whether you feel it or not.
Because at its deepest meaning,
love is the commitment to go the distance
no matter what befalls us.

Shrouded

Presence in my life,
long have we been shrouded from each other.
Only glimpses breaking through
to be gone in a fleeting moment.
Thank you for staying by me,
longing for me as much as
I have longed for you.
Blessed be.

INTRODUCTION

I was raised in a traditional family: two parents who stayed together, two boys and two girls. I was the oldest. We lived in a white suburb of Cincinnati. My parents were raised in upper middle-class families. We never rose to that echelon. It was a great disappointment to them that we were just middle class. I was also raised in an alcoholic household. My role was that of the hero child. I would try to make things go well in the household. I grew into adulthood way too soon.

I don't remember much about growing up until I was a teen. My dad's style of parenting was to tease. He did not know how to give a compliment. I don't remember my mom giving compliments, either. She was busy getting her master's degree so she could teach. Then, she worked, got involved with teaching organizations, and just wasn't around a lot to parent. The few times I remember her parenting, I was being castigated for expressing too much exuberance. I think I was loved. It may also be true that I just don't remember the good times.

This environment was not good for a sensitive child. My parents saw me as moody. By the time I was eleven, I was depressed. I don't remember when the depression started. Early in life is what my psyche tells me. I internalized the criticism I received at home, so I developed a strong inner critic which fed my self-loathing and shame for not being as perfect as I "should" have been.

I turned to church for comfort. There, I was told I was loved. I also learned that I was so wicked, god had to send his son to die for my sins. When I was eleven, the guilt this engendered brought me to born-again Christianity. For some reason, even though I was worthless, I was loved by god. However, god's love was dangerous. It could send you to a cross. I was sure if I wanted something, it wouldn't be god's will for my life. (For example, I desperately wanted to marry, but was sure god didn't want that for me).

But, I get ahead of myself.

Being born-again was supposed to bring you the fruit of the spirit: 22"love, joy, peace, patience, kindness, generosity, faithfulness, 23 gentleness, and self-control" (Gal. 5:22-23 NRSVue). It was not so for me. From junior high school to my junior year of college, I was deeply depressed. The cloud lifted a bit when I met Steve, the man who became my husband nine years after we met.

My first year out of college I lived with two friends. Steve was in Dayton, finishing his bachelor's degree. I had been attending a mainline protestant church since graduating from college. At the end of the year, both my roommates left for other adventures, and I needed a place to live. My church had what they called a "live-in" program, where a person would live with church members. Not only live with them, but be under their authority.

That is how I ended up in a cult. No one thought it was a cult; at least the members didn't consider it as such. It was only after I left that I realized I had been in a cult. Until then, this church was my life. I cut my previous friends out of my life for the good of my soul. That included Steve.

I had new friends. Lots of them. I had never had so many friends. We had a very active singles group. I was in leadership of the group for a few years. I sang in the choir and taught Sunday school. But there was a price to pay. The teaching in the cult was focused on helping people become like Jesus. Their way to achieve this was by the use of correction when a person was "in sin." This was especially true for the live-ins. We wrote daily notes to our live-in parents confessing our sins. And we lived where the head pastor thought we should. I think I was moved seven times in one year.

The second to last house I was in had a cat. It turns out I am very allergic to cats. Their presence could bring on an asthma attack. Now, there was a curious thing about this. Sometimes, when it was determined I was "in sin" and having an asthma attack, confessing that sin would break the attack. My besetting sins were jealousy and judgment.

When it was time for me to move, I was placed in another house with a cat. No amount of confession would help me breathe while I lived there. I was using my inhaler every five minutes. (It was supposed to be used every four hours). One night, I couldn't take it anymore. I packed a bag and walked out of the house where I was living. My body was telling me that this way of life was killing me. I also left more deeply convinced than ever of my worthlessness.

How do I know it was a cult? It was a closed system: us (the good ones) vs the others (those who had yet to see the light). I was under the authority of the leadership, and had to check in with them before I did anything, even go to a movie. Thus, I had given my will to another. Any impulse to depart the group was deemed deserting god's will for my life.

After my departure, the cult closed me off. I became the outsider who no longer followed the true way. Shunned. As the pastor commented, "I was like Jonah in the belly of the great fish. The longer I stayed away, the harder it would be to return." Yes, I was crazy enough to go back for an "exit" interview.

I did not return. It took a long time, but I am no longer plagued by asthma. However, the deep-seated depression is with me today. Now I have days of remission—more often than not. But depression is still my baseline affect, a daily struggle to keep my head above water.

My former friends took me back. Steve and I got back to together and married. I found a new church which worked for a while. One of the pastors, Pat Youngdahl, was instrumental in assisting me develop my own theology. Eventually. I knew I had to leave Christianity. The theology of a sacrificial death for the forgiveness of sins no longer made sense to me. I am now a Unitarian/Universalist where I can work on my salvation without fear and trembling (Phil 2:12).[1]

How did I make it so far into recovery? I had a lot of help from loving people (see acknowledgments). And I was resilient beyond all expectations. Then, there are the special people from One Spirit Learning Alliance. I have studied there for seven years: becoming ordained and gaining certificates in spiritual counseling. My involvement there has been a big part of my healing. Finally, with the help and love of Divine Writing Journey and Flower of Life Press, this book is coming to fruition. All have contributed to my healing.

I have also had loving support from my husband, Steve, and daughter, Carys. Even our furry ones, Sami and now Gala, have added to the healing atmosphere in our home.

---

1 Therefore, my beloved, just as you have always obeyed me, not only in my presence but much more now in my absence, work on your own salvation with fear and trembling, 13 for it is God who is at work in you, enabling you both to will and to work for his good pleasure. (Phil. 2:12-13 NRSVue).

Longing

As I look at my life, today.
What needs to go into the trash can
because it no longer serves me?
What vision am I holding for myself?

I imagine a wise woman who welcomes all and is a conduit of spirit for them. I want to continue to listen and recognize the voice of spirit, which is my own voice. I want to be the light of Holy Mystery, glowing softly, warmly.

I want to learn to recognize the critic that holds me back while, at the same time, accepting guidance without rebellion. To live my life by my values: compassion, acceptance, openness, and as a portal of wisdom with humility. To have a servant's heart without giving away (boo-hiss) pieces of myself. And I would gain recognition as a wise woman and an artist.

These are my hopes for you as you peruse this volume. May you find an outlet for your grief and pain. And may you find glimmers of faith that there is Holy Mystery who loves you beyond measure. May you laugh and cry; sorrow and rejoice. Because the light at the end of the tunnel is *not* an on-coming train, rather it is the glow of hope.

STARTING POINT

This section sets the stage for my ongoing struggle with depression and my desire to experience Holy Mystery.

Who Am I?

So, I'm not my thoughts.
Nor am I my feelings.
So who am I?
Or is it what am I?
"I am who I am" (Ex 3:14 NRSVue).
A child of the Most High;
home to the Holy Spirit;
a soul living the life of myself.

Sprite Wings

Uncanny Sprite peeks out through riotous curls
Joy-full, she spreads her wings;
secure, she soars, unfettered, unafraid.
Blindsided by friendly fire.
Dragged to earth.
"Why?"
"Go to the corner."
"But, why?"
"Don't you but me. Go!"
"Mm?"
Silence.
Crushed.
Confused.
Condemned.
Banished.
Then released.
But more canny,
sensitized to shifting currents,
receding into watchfulness.
Until,
she stopped coming out to play at all.
Haven in hiddenness.
Exorbitant price for safety.
Constrained with implacable resolve.
Guarded by fear and hopelessness.
Banished.
But not lost.
Biding her time,
she still peeks out.
Tests her wings, but secretly,
so no one can see.
Dreams of soaring
from her earthbound reality.
Sprite Wings, she's called.
And she loves earrings. That's how she sparkles.

Going to the corner was the punishment of choice for me. I would cry my heart out. Maybe that's why I don't remember being spanked. The corner didn't work for my brothers, so spanking was introduced. I would cry when my brothers were spanked.

Essence

So, I believe my essence is a lump of coal—not a soul.
A lump whose existence
can only be expunged by flame;
flame that will consume the whole organism.
But what if it is only a part?
Whence did it arise?
What does it hide?
Coal—created by extreme pressure,
the crucible of my life.
Coal—raw materials going through sea changes,
becoming hard and useful.
Not ugly at all.
Maybe, and I'm speaking from a faith perspective,
maybe the flame of love can transform the coal
into energy for the soul.

Letter From the Goddess

Dear child,
beautiful child,
full of compassion and grace.
How I have longed to hold you
and dry your tears.
Long have I watched you suffer.
You were not alone
although that is how you felt.
I can't tell you why
you had to experience so much pain.
It is for you to take the scraps of your life
and patch them into a full cloth.
All the pieces will have their place.

Response

I don't know how to embody this. I don't feel the comfort she offers. My chest hurts, my tears are unshed. Her offering is insufficient compared to the pain I have experienced. Decades of depression—of not knowing where to go and how to get there. My body reveals the rigidity I feel when in her arms. I am sad, but the tears still don't come. My eyes burn, my arms hug my body, protecting it from more pain.

The Cult

I was in a cult.
It wasn't all bad.
I had friends.
And purpose:
I was on a path to become
like Jesus.
But the price of conformity was too high.
My belief in my essential worthlessness was confirmed.
My body knew before my mind.
I got very sick
until I left.
I lost my friends.
I lost my god.
I lost my purpose.
The healing continues to this day.
But at last, I was free.

Open Hearts

Holy Spirit, thank You for your presence here.
May I open my heart to You,
knowing that Yours is open to me.
May I follow Your lead
in all my ways
through all my days.
Especially during this time we share.
Blessed be.
May it be so.

MORNING

Tallis's Canon[2]

All praise to thee my God this day,
for all thy blessings, come what may.
Keep me, O keep me from alarm,
enfolded in thy loving arms.

Plug In

Plug into the heartbeat **of the earth.**
Flow with its rhythms.
Listen to its voice.
Sing its song of joy,
that all may be well.

---

2 Thomas Tallis, "God Grant with Grace," 1567, lyrics by C. Coates.

Gāla

Sanctus mysterium,[3]
Gracious Companion.
Early morning vigil
walking Gala, the dog.
Listening to birdsong.
The woodpecker isn't up yet,
but the cardinals are
and so many others I don't know.
Silly me.
I rush to get back inside
rather than follow Gala's lead
to stay and listen for a while
and join my voice
to the greeting of the dawn.
Kyrie/Kyra eléison.[4]

Closer Than Breath

Belovèd, closer than breath;
Heartbeat of the universe.
I long to know Your presence
in my heart of hearts,
that I might follow You this day.
With thanksgiving for Your ever-present grace.
Blessed Be.

---

3 Holy Mystery.
4 Lord/Lady have mercy. I have added Lady to this cry, because Holy Mystery is neither.

Verdancy

Great Gardener,
Source of earth's fullness.
We are destroying this gift;
ignoring earth's pleas.
Forgive our chutzpah.
Give us eyes to see what we are doing,
that peace and verdancy would reign.
May it be so.

Bearings

Holy Comforter,
Divine Presence.
The energy in our world has shifted.
We need to regain our bearings,
trim our sails for the weather ahead.
Take time for the healing to gradually take hold,
for peace and acceptance to plant in our souls,
that a new way of life may blossom into being.
May it be so.

Salvation

Holy Redeemer,
Savior.
From what do we need to be redeemed?
From what can we be saved?
Our forgetfulness
of whose and who we are:
enfleshed spirit;
the hands of Holy Mystery.
Remind us at every moment
that we are in this together.
Kyra/Kyrie eléison.

Blues

The task before me is onerous in my sight.
Asking much of me I find difficult to give.
Yet, the work needs to be done.
I seek your wisdom, Most High,
accompanied by deep insight and love.
There is a blessing here, somewhere.
May I open to it through Your grace.
Blessed be.

Pathways

Holy Mystery,
ever present support.
I have been away too long,
finding other things to do
or nothing to do.
But it doesn't occur to me
to turn to You.
Teach me, Belovèd, to follow Your pathways,
that I might keep on the journey
without losing my way
May it be so.

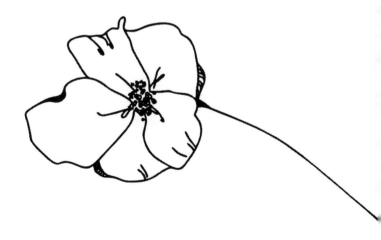

Retirement

I retired in January 2020, after fifty years of being an employee. For the last twenty of those years, I worked as a glorified data entry clerk at Xerox. Before that, I was an accounting clerk, a manager of a pizzeria, a cake decorator and lunch chef (my favorite job), and then spent several years keeping track of donations for a divinity school. The best part of the divinity school: I got to take classes.

I never had a plan for my life except to get ordained, which I eventually did when I was sixty-three. Oh, I also wanted to get married, which I did when I was twenty-nine. I was thirty-eight when I became a mother.

The retirement party was a big deal. My job had impacted a lot of people. Seventy people indicated they would attend. For a variety of reasons, I'd never had a real going away party from any of my places of employment. This one was very satisfying.

Holy Mystery,
Celebrant who rejoices with us.
Thank you for this day
where I was celebrated.
They clapped for me twice
I am grateful beyond words.
Thank you for a heart open to their praise.
Blessed be.

New Path

Sojourner,
Companion for the journey.
I start a new path today.
Retirement and I hope more.
May I sense Your guiding presence
and follow as You lead.
Blessings to You as You have blessed me
on this journey.
Amen.

Future Shock

Holy Presence, Comforter, and Guide.
After the party and applause,
the celebratory dinner,
there is the gaping maw of the future
awaiting my presence—
my choices
as well as the laundry, the dusting, the mopping—
possibility and boredom.
"I am learning every day to allow
the space between where I am, and
where I want to be to inspire me
and not terrify me."[5]

Morning Star

Lover, seen in the morning star,
You greet me as I rise.
Help me use this time
in communion with You,
that I will be attuned to Your voice
throughout the day.
Singing Your blessings.
Amen.

5 Tracee Ellis Roos in Alan D. Wolfelt, 2016, *Grief One Day at a Time,* Ft. Collins, CO: Companion Press.

Dry Bones

The hand of the LORD came upon me, and he brought me out by the spirit of the LORD and set me down in the middle of a valley; it was full of bones.[2] He led me all around them; there were very many lying in the valley, and they were very dry.[3] He said to me, "Mortal, can these bones live?" I answered, "O LORD GOD, you know."…[5] Thus says the Lord GOD to these bones: "I will cause breath[6] to enter you, and you shall live" (Ez. 37 :1-3, 5 NRSVue).

Great mystery of dry bones,
Breath of Life.
I am dry like these bones.
Breathe in me, and through me
Enliven me in all ways.
Dea/Deo Gratias.[7]

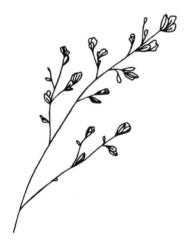

Surrender-Not

Mother Goddess,
Father God.
I wake up grumpy
I'm tired,
and haunted by troubling
dreams
where I am always wrong,
and being controlled by others.
At least they try—
but my will is strong
And I won't back down.
You know how I feel about
surrendering—not on my watch.
Yet letting each moment
be as it is—
that is a type of surrender.
May it be so.

---

6 Wind or spirit.

7 Thank you, goddess.

Demons Dissipated

This morning I want to wake up with, no—
actually, I don't want to wake up.
But if I must
I want depression to no longer weigh me down.
Is that true?
Depression is my invisibility cloak.
I hide behind it so no one can see
the deep pain, sadness, guilt, and shame
that are my constant companions.
So odd—depression as a protector
when it is, in itself, a tormentor.
This morning I want to wake up unencumbered.
Flying free, and reveling in it.
Until the tormentors have dissipated,
and the depression has run its course.

Trust Your Heart

"Your heart knows the way. Run in that direction," [8]
Holy Spirit, Love divine,
every morning is a gift
full of plans and surprises.
Times to be still, and
times to accomplish.
May I be sensitive to the present moment—
shunning despair when I don't know
what to do next.
Take a beat so that the next step
can become clear; even when that step is no step.
Trust the heart to know how to proceed.

---

8 Jalāl al-Dīn Muhammad Rūmī, "Your heart knows," Goodreads,
https://www.goodreads.com/quotes/9941552-. (accessed 8/7/2022).

Bask

Sacred One.
I greet You this morning.
A new opportunity to walk Your paths,
and bask in your love.
May I attune to the day's rhythm,
from task to bask to task, and finally
bask in Your presence with gratitude.
All done under the umbrella of Your love.
Blessed be.

Weaving

Sacred Mother,
Co-weaver of my life.
Draw from my heart Your gifts:
wisdom, compassion, hope, grace, and courage.
Together, we will interweave these threads with joy and peace.
Thus empowered, I will do my part to embrace the world with Love.
May it be so.
Blessed be.

INTIMATIONS OF HOLY MYSTERY

Before the Beginning

Before the beginning, Holy Mystery is.
Out of its own nature Creation becomes.
Holy Mystery shares its' Is-ness with all that is.
Holy Mystery is everywhere present.
But does that mean Holy Mystery is in all things?
A potter puts themselves into making the pot, but does not become
the pot.
Is there a Whom, beyond myself, to which I can connect?
The theist solution says, "Yes," and gives that Whom myriads of names.
If Holy Mystery does not exist as somehow separate, who am I
addressing when I pray?
Are spiritual practices not so much a reaching for the Other as they are a
tool for tuning our spirit to hear our own voice?
Are we left with the existential angst of being ultimately alone?

Bubbles

God is not the one who lays down the law.
Rather, the sacred is that which
bubbles up in joy, love, connection,
compassion, hope, presence, mystery, healing,
and peace.
And so, it is.

Holy Silence

Dynamic Creator
out of the abyss You called us.
Om.
Thus, the worlds began,
with Love everywhere present.
We can experience You in many ways,
but it is in the sound of sheer silence [9]
that we can hear Your voice.
Let us quiet our hearts and minds, and
open to the voice within.
Blessed Be.

Control

I don't think I love you, god.
Indeed, I don't even believe in you.
Because you aren't the god I want.
They say there is a god where "everything is in divine order,"
but that just doesn't make sense to me.
If you have that much control, what choice do I have?
What choice did Hitler, or Putin, or Jesus have?
I wish there were such a god. Then I could relax in its safety.
But life isn't safe, and I do have choice—although it is likely
circumscribed by chaos, chance, and the choices of others.
What then can we say?
Are we doomed because god isn't in control?
Or is something deeper going on?
If god isn't in control, what is its purpose?
It is the one in whom "'we live and move and have our being'"
(Acts 17:28 NRSVue).
And Its nature is Love.

---

9 "… and after the earthquake a fire, but the LORD was not in the fire, and after the fire
a sound of sheer silence." (1 Kings 19:12 NRSVue).

DNA

Holy Mystery,
Divine One to my forebears.
I carry within me
their hopes and dreams
Their pains and sorrows,
etched through shared DNA.
May my life bring closure to theirs.
Blessed be.

Haiku

Making sense of life
structure for the path ahead
Spirit breaks through the rules.

Sun rises, sun sets
the eternal web, dancing
butterfly kisses.

We do not prove God.
Sacrality is presence
enfolding us all.

Jesus' Prayer Adapted

Holy One, who is ever-present
Blessed be thy names.
Help us to make Your commonweal
the way of life for the whole cosmos.
Today, let us revel in Your grace.
Help us to see where we miss the mark,
responding to all hurtfulness with **compassion**.
Help us to seek and follow Your **lead**
Spreading love on all our paths.
For You are One
Who is forever more.
Amen.

SEHNSUCHT[10]

Searching

I've searched scripture.
I've gone on retreats.
I've prayed, meditated,
listened to the sheer silence.
I've besought Your presence all my life.
And I still haven't found what I'm looking for.

---

10 Jennifer Neyhart(2014), "CS Lewis on Sehnsucht Longing and Desire in *The Weight of Glory*," October 3, 2014, (Accessed 8//2/2022), https://www.jenniferneyhart.com/2014/10/c-s-lewis-on-sehnsucht-longing-and.html. "For (C.S.) Lewis, *Sehnsucht* was the sense of deep, inconsolable longing, yearning, the feeling of intensely missing something when we don't even know what it is."

Like the Wind

Sacred and Holy Mystery.
What is it like to feel Your presence?
I am not being facetious.
I get glimpses, afterward,
that something larger than I
has been present.
Like the wind.
I see the evidence of its existence
even if it is only the barest ripple.
Teach me to trust in Your presence
whether I feel it or not.
Kyrie/Kyra eléison

Mist

Holy Mystery,
enshrouded in mist.
What does Your voice sound like?
How do I know it's You I'm hearing?
My soul longs for Your touch;
my heart opens to receive You.
If you are heard in the silence,
then there's nowhere to go
to hear Your voice.
It is here.
It is now.
It is presence.
So many words.
So little faith.

Let God In

Holy Mystery,
called by myriads of names
What would it be like
to let You be **You** in my life?
I would know Your love surrounds me
and let Your love infuse me.
I would let Your wisdom guide me.
I would bask in Your presence
knowing that I am enfolded
in Your arms.
When fears assail me
I would find my courage in You.
"Surely goodness and mercy will follow me
all the days of my life,
and I shall dwell in the heart of the
Belovèd forever. Amen." [11]

11   Nan C. Merrill ([2007], 2016)). *Psalms for Praying. An Invitation to Wholeness.* (39)
London: Continuum Publishing, used by kind permission of Bloomsbury Publishing
Plc.

Eyes of Heaven

"Most Holy,
who am I to You?"
"My belovèd."
"Why?"
"Because you are."
"I am what?"
"My belovèd.
Whose heart is pure
and compassionate."
"This doesn't sound like me."
"How would you know?
You're not looking with the eyes of heaven."

Miracle

I don't know Holy Mystery,
despite my longing.
I only know that the world is a miracle:
the verbena, the fox, the barking dog.
Without Holy Mystery,
nothing would make sense.
Stars, oceans, and quiet communion
of humans, and dolphins,
the soft white pine trees,
the rain.
What doesn't make sense is
the violence, destruction, and climate change.
Or, maybe those are the results of our
chutzpah—self-centeredness—
our failure to seek Holy Mystery.
Our power for destruction
is greater than we know.
Kyrie/Kyra eléison.

Glimpses

Loving Presence,
infuse me with Your love, I pray.
But, I fear this prayer will go unanswered
for unknown reasons.
I have been alone so long.
Why should now be any different?
Glimpses come to me.
Noticing, like Jacob, after the fact.[12]
What would different look like?
Feel like?
Be like?
Kyrie/Kyra eléison.

Breathe Most Deeply

"Then the Lord God formed man from the dust of the ground, and
breathed into his nostrils the breath of life; and the man became a living
being" (Gen 2:7 NRSVue).
Breathe most deeply
Mingling my breath with Yours, Most High.
Deep within
my heart longs for Your touch.
"Deep calls to deep" (Ps 42.7a. NRSVue).
"Out of the depths I cry to you, O Lord,
Lord, hear my voice" (Ps 130 1-2a. NRSVue).
"Your voice do I hear.
I wrap you in my arms of love.
Rest in me and
breathe most deeply."
Blessed be.

---

12 "Surely the Lord is in this place—and I did not know it!" (Gen 28: 16b. NRSVue).

Cry

"A voice says, 'Cry out!'
And I said, 'What shall I cry'" (Is 40:6 NRSVue)?
"I am belovèd of Holy Presence
Brought forth in love,
shining as a lantern of hope and peace
Made steady by grace."
Enveloped in joy, I make my way home.
Blessed be.

VALLEY OF THE SHADOW OF DEATH

This section is about facing my depression. And, I have to warn you, it's not pretty. For I have looked into the eyes of death, and considered succumbing to its call. I have also considered rejecting belief in any sort of god. There are not really any answers, but perhaps it's the questions that matter.

So, hold my hand as we take this journey. It's a rough road. But rest assured, we will make it through to the other side. Please know that you are not alone as you read this section.

Unending Pain

How long, O LORD, how long
will my existence be a burden to me?
I live without hope.
Fear is my constant companion.
Busy-ness and sleep are my only refuge.
But, busy-ness is hard to maintain.
Pain visits me in my dreams.
I am always wrong, or behind, or lost
Fueled by grief.
Whence comes my help?
I don't think help is coming.
Alone—all alone
No still-small voice whispering
endearments,
solace,
acceptance,
love.
All is vanity—all is dross.
Momentary flashes of light
are consumed by the unending night.
If there is light
what good is it,
always swallowed up by unending pain?

Bleakness

Holy Mystery.
I have so little to offer:
A broken heart,
a depressed spirit,
an unquenchable longing for Your touch.
And, in my bleakness,
I don't recognize Your voice.
Kyra/Kyrie eléison.

Dukkha

All is *dukkha:*[13]
Impermanence.
Transient except for the present moment.
Although it, too, fades into the next one.
This is a true letting go of:
all things,
all relationships,
all beliefs,
all traditions…
All life is ephemeral.

---

13 Elizabeth Tarbox, 2015, "Wisdom From our Sources: All is Dukkha," http://www.cascadeuu.org/wp-content/uploads/2015/09/Wisdom-from-our-Sources-July-3.pdf, (Accessed 5/27/2022). Defining dukkha as impermanence.

Blockage

Ganesha.[14]
Although we don't know each other,
I turn to you in my need.
I have heard you are the god of new beginnings and breaking
down obstacles.
I have locked away my heart
in my fear of being hurt.
I'm like a sprite whose wings were
ripped off when she was very young.
Is there hope for me?
Can I grow back my wings,
that I might soar with the eagles?
How might I find keys to unlock my heart
and unburden my soul?
Thank you for hearing my cry.
Blessed Be.

---

14   The Rev. Dr. Sushmitta Mukherjee, email to author, 9/4/2022, "The remover of
obstacles, or one who brings success to one's quests."

Hear My Cry

Hear my cry, Holy Mystery.
Attend to my prayer.
For my enemies have pitched
their tents in the midst of the
inner city.
They destroy all that gets in their way.
Their numbers are legion.
"It's hard to fight an enemy who has outposts in your head."[15]
Can we open negotiations?
Who will speak for me?
Words are dust in my mouth.
Holy Mystery, have mercy on me.
Lead me through this dismal valley,
that I might hope in You again.

Habit

I am more than the sum of my parts.
But the parts are what I wear
to navigate the treacherous ways of life.
Depression is a habit I wear.
A habit I practice.
A safe haven,
or so I think.
A method devised by my young mind
to make sense of the world in which I lived.
But the habit feels like a second skin.
Taking it off would be like a 3rd degree burn.
I imagine the healing from that to be more painful
than the pain of wearing the tattered rags
of this old habit.

---

15 Sally Kempton, "Cutting Loose," Esquire Magazine, July 1970.

Bondage

Ruach Ha'Kodesh,[16]
Bestower of life.
I come to you empty
Bereft of energy, love, and mercy
for myself.
My eyes are shadowed by bleakness
Whither is my hope?
Whence shall come my salvation.
Breathe through me Breath of Life
Enable me to untangle these bonds
without fighting their presence in my life.
Dea/Deo Gratias.

Morass

Mother Earth,
ever present, ever loving.
I've been in a foul disposition
wanting some ease in the deluge of days.
Overwhelmed by the basic needs,
how am I to find the time
to serve beyond the little bits
I do at home?
And the days are so heavy.
What respite?
I know of none
but to continue slogging through the
morass.

---

16 Sacred Breath of God.

Shame

Buried deeply in my heart.
Hiding from the light
Masquerading as depression.
They look the same from the outside.
And I act the same:
shut down,
unable to adequately function.
Frozen in place.
Lost in myself.
Lost to myself.
Its companion is anxiety
whose antidote is faith.
Faith that being myself
is a blessing to be shared.
Kyrie/Kyra eléison.

Luffing

Holy Seafarer,
Keeper of leviathan and minnows.
My sails are luffing in the wind.
How am I to get back on course?
Do You know where we're going?
Do You have a star map to guide me?
A sextant to assist in navigation to
the port of Your choosing?
Lead me to that shore where
I can flourish in your grace and presence.
May it be so.

Oasis

Baa…where are they?
Maa…or that young man with the staff?
How could they leave me here,
stuck in this brush?
I hear wolves approaching,
carrion birds circling.
Whence comes my help?
Wait, there on the horizon
two-legged ones,
they chase the wolves,
but seem intent on lamb stew.
Then another, implacable,
steals me away for his own purposes:
sacrifice.
But I'm blemished, inappropriate.
He lets me go
to wander the waste places
alone, but free.
Surely there's an oasis out there—
somewhere.

St. Eeyore

From St. Eeyore the dysthymic.
All days are gloomy
no matter what is in the sky.
Expect the worst and you won't be surprised.*
Because the tail is likely to get lost again.
And friends don't really know how to help—
because there is no help for it.
But you still show up,
and sometimes, there are glimmers of hope.

*The concept of expecting the best does not occur to St. Eeyore, and being
surprised by joy is quickly buried in the gloom.

Suicide

I thought longingly of the pills downstairs;
Saw myself take them—
But then I would cry for help.
Just what the hospital needs:
A suicide attempt on their hands.
So, I went to bed.
Today is not quite so bad.
The impulse to self-destruct has passed.
Where did it go?
Will it come back?
(Of course it will).
What was the gift in that moment
When I contemplated suicide?
I was expressing my longing for the essence of Peace.

Pitsville

Agent of Change,
Calm Spirit in the storm.
I visited the pit, again.
The outside is so fraught with fear and confusion.
My interior cluttered and askew.
I am needful enough—but am I brave enough
to reach for Your hand already outstretched to greet me?
Please, help me on my way to the next vista.
Kyrie/Kyra eléison.

Calamity

Sanctus mysterium.
One who hears the cries of the world.
What does one pray in the midst of calamity?
"Save me from this hour?" (John 12:27 NRSVue).
Didn't work for Jesus.
What will come, will come.
The promise is we will not be alone[17]
Then why do I feel alone so often?
What good is the promise if
the goods don't come through?
Kyrie/Kyra eléison.

---

17 "Even though I walk through the darkest valley,[d] (Or the valley of the shadow of death) I fear no evil, for you are with me" (Ps 23:16 NRSVue).

Pain

Open your heart, they say.
But there is so much pain within.
Opening up would only let in more pain,
wouldn't it?
There are no guarantees that the flow would go the other way—
that the pain would drain
and love would enter.
They say the love is already there.
Then why do I feel only pain?
What kind of god is it that lets so much pain abound?
They say god is feeling our pain with us.
So what?
And how do they know?
Who the hell are "they" anyway?
And what kind of god feels the pain
rather than expels it?
They must have walked this path before,
those who are not spouting platitudes.
And the God who is there—
the God who is everywhere present—
is in the heart where it has always **been**—
suffering with us
and filling the empty places with love.

Rage

Seeing red.
Not my favorite color.
Not my favorite feeling.
Indeed, I try not to feel it at all.
But it festers—
and burns—
and inhibits my growth.
How to process it
without creating a conflagration
that takes everything down?
My preference—
keep it to myself.
Then only I get burned
and fail to fulfill my calling.
Kyrie/Kyra eléison.

So, what to do with anger? Expressing it indiscriminately is indulgence and can damage the other. Suppressing it judges it as inappropriate and damages the self. The middle road is to accept it. Listen to what it has to say. Wait for what's next. Use its energy for the benefit of all.

What God?

So, who is god to you?
Silence.
Then a few mumbled words about Tao, and om,
and then…Presence.
 But if god is presence,
absence is what I feel.
God goes before, god is between, god within.
No, only absence for me.
Deserted long ago by the born-again god
who came bearing gifts, but none for me,
still grieving its loss.
But he never came through with the fruit—
Well, maybe self-control, perhaps patience and kindness, at least I try.
But never the big ones: Love, Joy, Peace—certainly not goodness,
faithfulness, and gentleness.
My fault, no doubt.
Existential angst, then, my only refuge?
Cold, harsh emptiness my only reality?
Absence, indeed.
Mea culpa.[18]

---

18 All my fault.

Feeding the Flames

Holy Oneness,
I am in a foul disposition.
The cause isn't the issue.
It's my choice to continue feeding the flames
rather than speak my truth.
I am passive-aggressively maintaining silence,
holding a grudge.
While the one to whom I am reacting
goes on blithely,
unaware of the hurt their words invoked in me.
Speak, then, and be done with it—except,
if I speak, I will no longer be right.
Kyra/Kyrie eléison.

Sadness

Holy Mystery
Today, I woke as usual
with sadness in my heart.
I don't know why I choose that.
Or does it choose me?
It free floats through my day,
showing up whenever I take a break.
"Hello, there you are.
What do you have to say to me?"

A Problem

Holy Mystery,
if I am not a problem to be solved,
who am I? What am I?
There are not enough kudos in the world
to offset my belief that I'm no good.
The antidote reportedly is:
be present to what is.
Well, what is, sucks!

Don't Tell Me What To Do!

Mysterious presence,
still, small voice.
I come to you as
Queen of the "Yes, buts"
and, "I don't wannas."
It's not as though I don't know what
would be a good use of my time.
But there is this little one inside
who has their feet firmly planted
and won't budge.
"Don't tell me what to do!"

Divine Shepherd

Divine Shepherd,
Mysterious Presence.
"All we like sheep have gone astray;
We have all turned to our own way" (Is 53:6a. NRSVue).
Yet You remain steadfast
in Your love for us.
Ever present, ever faithful.
Ever ready to carry us home.

Belovèd Physician

Divine Healer,
Source of all understanding.
I bring to You my pain.
What is it trying to tell me?
What salient points am I ignoring?
What experiences have not been processed?
I seek Your clarity and wisdom,
belovèd physician.
Dea/Deo Gratias.

Say, Yes

To what can I say, "yes," today?
To what do I want to say yes?
When I look at a day
all I think about is what to do.
And then I come up against
the wall of not knowing what or
not wanting to.
I'll pause and wait for intuition to kick in.
But so often I get stuck in
the loop of knowing and wanting,
and my mind scatters
And I take a nap.
Kyra/Kyrie eléison.

Have Mercy

"Have mercy on me, O God,
according to your steadfast love,
according to your abundant mercy,
blot out my transgressions" (Ps 51:1 NRSVue).
Deep within,
I still believe in the
angry god
ever ready to pounce
to devour me
at the slightest provocation.
(Or am I the one who pounces)?
Nonetheless, this god is indifferent to my cries.
The Prime Mover
who has turned away from creation,
leaving me bereft.
Whence comes my help?
From the Belovèd
Who is the keeper of
"your going out and your coming in
from this time on and forevermore" (Ps 121:8 NRSVue).

Depression

Depression, my old friend
You've come to walk with me again.
Why are you visiting?
Whose emotions am I feeling?
I've survived so often
and never really know how I manage.
But it will pass.
If I let it—somehow.
But while it's here
hHow then shall I live
when I wish to be dead?
What does it mean to be present
to this moment
when it feels horrible?
Whence comes my help?
Is help even coming?

Despair

Every day, I don't know what to do
or which way to go.
I'm a professional whiner,
"woe is me."
That is my baseline affect.
Yet, somehow I move.
I don't know how.
Left to myself, I would sleep all day.
Or, even worse—
cash in all my chips.
I'm not playing this game anymore.
I want out.

Death Wish

I am flatlining.
Not dead.
Rather lacking any desire
to live.
I have filled my life with things to do
and want to do none of it.
Why is that?
What is wrong with me?
What is right with me?
What is my deepest longing?
Is it to be dead?
No.
But I don't know what it is anymore.

The Deal

So, here's the deal.
Whoever you are.
I hate being myself
and being with myself.
I hate having to make decisions.
I have things galore
but they are a burden.
It is said if you live with less clutter
you will live longer.
Is living longer my goal?
Sometimes, not so much.

Faith

Have mercy on me, Belovèd,
for I am full of fear and trepidation.
The path ahead is shadowed.
The light in me only illuminates
the next step.
Faith, then, would be taking that step
without knowing for certain where it leads.
And trusting that the light I see in the distance
is not an oncoming train.

On Faith

I have been struggling with the concept of faith. Although I am a good theologian, without faith, I am a clanging gong. I have experienced an epiphany around this issue. It starts with Anne LaMott's quote, "I do not understand at all the mystery of grace—only that it meets us where we are but does not leave us where it found us."[19] This is something in which I have faith. My faith is in the process at work in the world, a process of cause and effect but much more. I have faith in the presence of Holiness, everywhere and at all times, especially within ourselves. There is no place where Holiness is not present—whether we feel it or not. And I have faith that Holiness goes before us, calling us into relationship with all that is. "For in Love's heart forevermore my dwelling place shall be; and in my heart forevermore Love's dwelling place shall be."[20]

---

19 Anne LaMott, e-mail to author, 8/3/2022.
20 James Leith Macbeth Bain, "Brother James Air," 1915. Lyrics adapted by C. Coates.

Pisspot

The Pisspot is my friend.
She saves me from unwelcome commitments,
feeds me chocolate sauce and ice cream every night.
Helps me hide in plain sight.
Let's me join the church
of sleeping in on Sunday.
She holds
anger, jealousy, self-pity.
But mostly anger,
the deep, cold, hard kind.
So hard, only the strongest acid
could make a dent, and maybe not even then.
And what of the Sprite?
Locked away in a closet,
dank and dismal.
Who is it that fears the closet
but fears the light more?
I don't think it's the Sprite.
She would love the light.
So, I'd rather be dead.
What part is that?
Despairing,
Overwhelmed,
Despondent
I'd rather rot than be free.

Prison

Prison of my own making,
walls of hurt and fear.
Sometimes a small window appears;
a bit of light–a bit of possibility
brightens the dark interior.
More often the walls close in.
I call for help–but no one hears–
the walls are too thick.
Surely someone must have a key–
and then I see
there's no door, no lock.
The only hope–enlarging
the window when it appears.
But it turns out this takes
me to another prison–
perhaps more spacious–
with more possibility–
but a prison, nonetheless.
Is the only way out death?

Bottomless Pit

Holy Mystery
Here I am, again, in a bottomless pit
without a chance of climbing out.
Above me, an impenetrable cloud
Guilt and self-hatred pressing me
down deeper.
Hopelessness, loneliness, so bleak—
where are you god?
I hear it said that you are with me in the pit.
But I can't hear you or sense your presence.
The walls are closing in—
it's getting harder to breathe.
Why is life so hard?
Then, I sense a possibility.
If the walls get close enough
I can align my body horizontally,
so I can shimmy up the wall.
Do I have the will?
Do I have the strength?
Or will I slip back down
and be crushed?

Wasteland

Not to compete with T. S. Eliot,
but my own experience—
a vast wasteland,
deep within,
barren,
silent,
life?
Desiccated:
hot wind by day,
frozen at night.

Ruled by a sovereign
wearing a tarnished and damaged crown;
its base made of thorns.
Deaf and blind to other possibilities,
for there is nothing real but the wasteland.

Blinded by the Light

Holy of holies,
I don't have anything to say, really.
I am worn out from the day,
ready for sleep.
Is this all there is?
One damn thing after another?
A permanent sleep doesn't sound so bad.
I can escape from the pain of being me.
What reason can I manufacture
for coming into the light?
Blinded by the light.
How can I see my way?
Do you happen to have sunglasses?

Nutsies

A trip to the deep nutsies
where life is not worth living.
Yet the heart beats on
Wiser than the thought that
death is preferable.
Deeper than feelings of despair.
Whence comes my hope?
From deep within
and far off.

So, how do I process all this pain? Why am I still here? The medical profession has certainly played a part in my survival. More importantly, there have been caring people who were there for me when I was in meltdown. Beyond that, I seem to have the gift of resilience, or maybe they were miracles. Even when I was at my worst, I managed to survive. Perhaps these writings played a part. When I emptied my heart of the pain, I was able to take the next step. I would say I felt tenderized by the process.

INTERLUDE

Snowfall

Snow outside my window makes me happy.[21]
Freezing cold can make me blue.
Put a fire in the ingle.
Warmth surrounds and satisfies.

I have just one thing to give You.
It's my heart now opened wide.
Will you tune it to your measure?
Our harmonious diapason fills the skies.

Begotten

Of Mystery's Love begotten,[22]
evolution on the wing.
Light of light beams through creation.
Breathing life in everything.
We are bearers of this holy light.
Called to shine, called to sing.
Evermore and evermore.
Amen.

---

21 John Denver, "Sunshine on My Shoulders," lyrics by C. Coates.
22 Aurelius Clemens Prudentius, circa 400 CE, lyrics by C. Coates.

Light of Light

Light of light,
Keeper of my soul.
May my light shine
with gentle, steady rays
that neither blind nor burn.
Like an oil lamp, properly trimmed,
with fuel sufficient for the day.
Blessed be.
Dea/Deo Gratias.

Particles in Waves

"God is light" (I John 1:5a. NRSVue).
Light presents as particle and wave.
Matter presents as particle and wave.
How could it be otherwise?
Creation's source is God's self—*creatio ex deo*[23]
Thus, we are the particles
in the waves of love.
Imago Dei.[24]

---

23 For more information about *creatio ex deo*: (creation out of God's own nature) Bill
Vallicella, 2016, "Creation ex Nihilo or ex Deo," Maverick Philosopher, 10/28/2016,
https://maverickphilosopher.typepad.com/maverick_philosopher/2016/10/creation-ex-
nihilo-or-ex-deo.html (Accessed 8/7/2022).
24 In the image of God.

Magick

"Make a joyful noise to the LORD, all the earth" (Ps. 100:1 NRSVue).
For mystery is afoot, and magick[25] is everywhere.
With light, love, and peace in its train—
even amidst the discord.
We are one in Spirit although we disagree.
May our hearts open to each other
so that light, love, and peace
become our way in the world.
Blessed be.

In the Beginning: Light

In the beginning,
The LORD created light,
and it was good.
From that light, all things came to be
each holding a bit of the light within.
We are light bearers
Our calling is to let that light shine.
May it be so.
Blessed Be.

---

25   For more information about Magick: Catherine Beyer, 2019, "Alternative Religions," Learn Religions, 1/25/2019, https://www.learnreligions.com/magic-and-magick-95856, (Accessed 9/23/2022).

Heart Blessing

We are sojourners in this world.
Our first home, a mother's womb,
our final one, a mystery.

And in between times we seek a sense of being at home:
in ourselves, our families, our world.
Flashes of fulfillment come in ways peculiar to each of us.
And, sometimes, we find a place where we experience that
warmth, acceptance, and contentment associated with being
"at home."

May your heart be such a place.
It is a sacred space, where love is always present,
where the lights of compassion, hope, and faith will shine,
even during times of confusion or loss.
Within its doors, may rest, refreshment, and renewal
be experienced in abundance,
providing haven and succor for life's journeys.
Blessed be.

In The Guest House,[26] Rumi calls us to welcome whatever shows up each day—not grudgingly, but with joy. This house is a metaphor for our heart, where we can choose how to respond to that which is brought into our life. This blessing, written originally for a housewarming, can be interpreted as a blessing of our hearts.

---

26 Jalal ad-Din Muhammad Rumi, https://www.thepoetryexchange.co.uk/the-guest-house-by-rumi, (Accessed 8/25/2022).

Womb

In the beginning was the womb.
And the waters of life gushed forth.
And life gave birth to life,
growing in complexity,
always seeking a return home
to the heart of God/ess.[27]
The journey nurtured by her breasts;
supported by his arms.
Grace offered in the possibilities of each moment.
Companionship in the communion of other seekers.
Solace in the wonder and beauty of creation.
Grace is not always sufficient to ward off the worst.
But it is always present,
striving for cosmos in the midst of chaos.

Spectrum

Out of darkness
came a beautiful light,
full spectrum,
shimmering with love.
Each spark glowing brightly,
and shining forth from each face.
Blessed be.

---

27 Rosemary Radford Ruether created the word God/ess to desexualize references to God.

Gaia

The Earth is my mother
who has blessed me with life.
Blessed be she.

The Earth is my shepherd
who has nourished me with good things,
and watched over my paths.
Blessed be she.

The Earth is my lover
who invites me to share intimacy, connection, love.
Blessed be she.

What can separate me from Earth's love?
From her I arose, to her I will return.
And she is with me all my days.

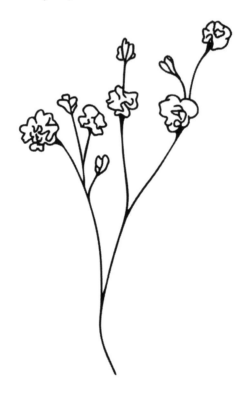

Mother God

First there was the warrior god,
bigger than we are,
who could go forth
and beat the god of our enemies,
thus, enabling us to destroy our enemies as well.

Then the dying god.
Dying for our sins,
or the earth's renewal,
or for some other damn purpose.
Life arising out of a required death.
As though our mother's birth pangs were insufficient
to bring forth abundant life.

But lost in the mist is the Mother God,
tender and fierce,
enfolding and releasing.
Whose tears water the earth
bringing forth life and love—her joy.
Please, Mother God,
Teach me faith in You.

The Underworld

"You don't believe in the Goddess, you experience her. Look into the mirror of the Goddess, and you see yourself."
A visit to the underworld
where Mother Gaia works her magic,
weaving evolution into the fabric of our days.
"Be still," she said.
"I love you."
"Be well."
We embraced, then performed *gassho rei*.[28]
And when I looked in her face,
I saw myself.[29]

---

28 Bowed from the waist with our hands pressed together.
29 Phyllis Curott, e-mail from author, 7/5/2022.

Blessing of the Day

Blessed Light, blessed Dark,
Holy Womb which births us each day.
In the midst of this chaos,
I notice the orchid in my window;
the still bare tree branches outside;
the shy sun making an appearance.
Grateful for the life into which I am born,
I rest in thee.
Dea/Deo Gratias.

Grace

Grace is an everywhere and everywhen possibility.
It is a way of seeing what is with humility.
It is Holy Mystery's way of tapping us on the shoulder.
"See me. See what I see."
For we have a view of things
but Holy Mystery has view.[30]

---

30 Madeleine L'Engle., "View," Quotefancy.com, n.d, https://quotefancy.com/
quote/999924/Madeleine-L-Engle-I-have-a-point-of-view-You-have-a-point-of-view-
God-has-view.

Gifts

Sanctus Mysterium,
Light of my life,
providing wisdom, warmth, and beauty.
Thank you for this glorious day.
This precious gift which lasts such a short time.
May I revel in the grace made present in you;
expand with joy that you have so blessed me.
I am God's gift to me.
I am God's gift in me.

Gratitude

Mystery Most Holy,
Sacred Presence.
Thank you for this day.
For the rain on my newly planted flowers.
For the extra sleep this morning
while waking up in time for meditation.
May gratitude continue to fill my heart
as I travel through the day.
Blessed be.

Tao

In the beginning was Tao.
Everything, yet No Thing.
Pure energy burst into form
that longs for return to source.
Tao is a way, a perspective.
Live in Tao faithfully
following the natural way of things.

Timing

It was all in the timing.
I "happened" to decide to water some flowers.
I "happened" to look up.
And there it was,
a beautiful hummingbird
checking out our coral bells.
Serendipity is a wonderful thing—a gift.
Unless, of course, you're in the wrong place
at the wrong time.
Then we call it bad luck.
Or sometimes god's will.
I don't believe Holy Mystery
sends ill will.
Even though bad things sometimes happen to good people.

Cat Feet

At times, depression rolls in on little cat feet,
appearing without notice,
pouncing at will.
In faith I say,
it will depart in its own time,
like the fog that disperses in the presence of the sun.

Starting a Sharing Session

Holy Spirit
Thank you for your presence here.
May we open our hearts to you
Knowing that yours is open to us.
May we follow your lead
In all our ways
Through all our days.
Especially during this time we share.
A' Ho.
May it be so.

HOW THEN SHALL WE LIVE?

How Then Shall We Live?

"Why do bad things happen to good people?"
Why do things happen at all?
Is there an ultimate plan,
and we're pawns in a cosmic game?
Is there only chance?
Does Holy Mystery play a part?
And how do we know if a thing is good or bad?
Or just a thing,
and our actions turn it into
a blessing, a curse, or something else entirely?
There are no guarantees as life happens.
So, how then shall we live?

Foreboding

Whence comes this all-encompassing feeling of foreboding?
It catches me unawares
and takes over.
I want to slink away and hide.
But where would I go?
I can't get away from myself.
What hope can You offer?
"I lift up my eyes to the hills—
from where will my help come?
My help comes from the LORD
who made heaven and earth" (Ps. 121:1-2 NRSVue).
In thee will I rest.
May it be so.
Blessed be.

Instrument of Peace

Holy Mystery
Keeper of my soul.
May my life be an outpouring of your love
so that I am an instrument of your peace
through which your voice sings,
always.
Blessed be.

Let It Be

Let it go—no,
Let it be.
Not Paul McCartney
But a call to relax—
Rest in the Holy One.
Let life unfold before me.
My job is to step onto the path
and follow the leading of the light.
May it be so.

Architect

Divine architect,
Creator of all that is.
"In all things God works for good…" (Rom 8:28 NRSVue).
May I be a willing apprentice
that I might learn the art
of being like You.
Blessed be.

Dreamer

Holy Messenger,
as complex and beautiful
as a dream catcher.
Help me trust my dreams
and pursue them with holy zeal.
So that cosmos might be made from
the chaos of my life.
Abiding in you as you abide in me.
In the name of Holy Mystery,
Blessed be.

Co-Creators

Holy Mystery,
Loving Presence.
Another day to choose
my way of life.
Do I lead from my heart or my head?
Do I need to choose between them?
"What about me?" my body cries.
Oh, yes, the body has a say in this process.
But, without being steeped in You
Are they even trustworthy?
"Yet you have made them a little
lower than God, and crowned them with glory and honor"
(Ps 8:5 NRSVue).
So, we do bring ourselves to the decision matrix
those things with which you have gifted us.
Indeed, we are co-creators with the divine,
called to make cosmos out of chaos.

Let Go—Let God

"Let go—let god."
I say, **"Let go of what?"**
Fear;
control;
insistence that things be;
different than they are;
bottled up feelings,;
demand that my way
is the only way.
I say, **"Let god what?"**
God is neither a spit guard
keeping me safe from the "slings and arrows of outrageous fortune,"[31]
nor a butler cleaning up after me.
Let god be God.
Who "bore you on eagles' wings and brought you to myself" (Exodus 19:4b NRSVue)
Supporting, loving,
bringing peace, hope, and insight.
The continual presence of grace.
And perhaps, preparing a table
before me that I might be nourished
by the Most High.

---

31   William Shakespeare, Hamlet, 3.1.58.

GPS

Be yourself, they say.
Be who you are meant to be.
How do I know who that is?
And who says?
Some have said
it's our soul that has the GPS (God's Perennial inSight).
There is a map (or maps) over which we have some influence.
But, if I don't know where I am going,
how do I input a destination?
In faith, I take the next step and trust the GPS
to redraw the map if I have gone astray.

Contractor

Holy Mystery,
ever-present with a listening ear.
I bring to you my broken heart
with little faith that it can be mended.
And yet, it is your dwelling place.
Do you have a contractor on staff?
One that can do the needed renovations
to make it a habitable home for you,
Most Holy?
"How lovely is your dwelling place"—(Ps 84:1a NRSVue)
and, thy dwelling place is within my heart.
Blessed Be.

Demands

I hammer at your door,
screeching for an explanation.
Why is life so hard?
Why are you so enigmatic?
"Dear one. Be at peace.
I am a mystery you don't have to solve."
Grr...what kind of answer is that?
I want to understand.
"In time, bit by bit,
until you come home to Me."

Believing

Out of the depths do I cry to You,
Holy, Wholly One (WHO).
I am heart sick, with no sense of your presence.
If my faith depended on such feelings
I would never address you again.
But,
I believe in the sun, even in the darkness.
I believe in God, even if God is silent.
I believe in compassion, even when it must remain hidden.[32]

---

32 Anonymous, Everett Howe, 2021 "I Believe in the Sun, Part V: The Source,"
Humanistseminarian.com, 4/4/2021, https://humanistseminarian.com/2021/04/04/i-
believe-in-the-sun-part-v-the-source/.

Respite

Holy Father,
Gracious Mother.
I thank you for your care of me.
That I've managed to survive
the hills and valleys of my life.
So many times, I'm barely dragging my sorry ass
through the swamp.
At least that's how it feels.
When will I reach a blessed garden of respite?
Such a joy that would be.
Deo/Dea Gratias.

Befuddled

Sacred Mother of us all.
I come to another day
befuddled and pulled
every which way.
Thank you for this day,
come what may.
Even in the midst of
confusion and anxiety,
may I find peace.
Dea/Deo Gratias.

Another Day

Sacred Mother of us all.
You have gifted me with another day.
May I listen for your call
to follow your paths
so that, come what may,
I will abide in your grace, and
and act with your wisdom
Sowing love and peace.
Blessed Be.

The Titmouse

Lover of Mary and Martha (Luke 10:38-42 NRSVue).
Still presence.
I am busy with many things
Exhausted with doing.
Then I saw the tufted titmouse,
listened to their song.
For a moment I was outside of my lists
Captured by wonder and joy.
Dea/Deo Gratias.

Keys

What is the key to my heart?
Is there a magic one to keep the monster within?
Another to free the sprite?
Are they in the same cell?
Of course, they are,
because I'm the cell.
And I'm the key to my own spirituality;
my own pathway to myself,
which is also the key to the Holy One—goodness, essence, freedom,
peace, and joy.

Eagles' Wings

"But those who wait for the LORD shall renew their strength;
they shall mount up with wings like eagles;
they shall run and not be weary; they shall walk and not faint" (Is 40:31
NRSVue).
Even when I am dead weight
over-burdened by life.
Help me to accept what is,
and relax under your careful watch,
for even "darkness is as light to you" (Ps 139:12c. NRSVue).

Puzzles

Holy, ever-present mystery,
I bring to you the bits and pieces of my life.
Like working a jigsaw puzzle,
we sort through them
to see what we might create.
The puzzle's pattern grows as we work.
A picture begins to take shape,
then new pieces appear.
How will we make them fit in?
Do some pieces need to be removed?
Together, we will find the patterns
in this appearing chaos called my life.

Be Glad

Holy Mother,
Sacred Mystery.
"This is the day that the LORD has made;
let us rejoice and be glad in it" (Ps 118:24 NRSVue).
Is it a choice?
Can I rise above the megrims
(or would the action be to subvert—go beneath them)?
Acknowledge their presence;
listen for any message they might have for me?
Listen more deeply to the still sound of silence
where I might hear your voice.

Possibilities

Holy Spirit,
Daily Presence.
I turn to you for guidance.
My days are so full of needs;
my response is lethargy.
Help me break through this miasma
that blinds my sight, and
leaves me enervated.
Not so that I respond with busy-ness.
Rather that I stay open to the possibilities of each moment.
Doing what is needful.
And even more, being one who is a channel
for healing and peace.
Dea/Deo Gratias.

Change

Holy Mystery,
I've written all these prayers
beseeching one thing or another
thinking to influence you to change my life.
But I heard today a truth.
It is I who needs changing
so that I can
choose your way, wisdom, and light.
May it be so.

Light on the Path

To One who goes before us,
lighting our path.
Please, give me a heart to discern
the best possible choice,
always knowing You will be there
whatever I choose.
Assure me, comfort me, and
let Your healing spirit encompass me.
Dea/Deo Gratias.

To Be

Loving Presence,
who gifts me with this day.
Forgive my ingratitude,
and my bleak perspective.
I would walk in your ways,
yet I am weighted down with "to-dos."
They have their place,
but more vital are the "to-bes."
To be
responsible,
loving, and
open,
listening for your voice always.

Persona

Holy Mystery.
Through all my prayers
I've missed a salient point.
I want You to make me a better person.
I want to be liked as the one that shows up.
Persona: wise and wonderful.
In reality, that's not Your wheelhouse.
I am already a pure soul whom You
love no matter what.
The persona needs to relax
so the "real" me that is You
shines through.
Blessed be.

Hands-on God

To: God/ess or someone else.
I want to have faith in a hands-on god.
In the thick of things,
always pulling for the best
possible outcome.
Maximizing profits if you will.
A process God/ess?[33]
Faith is more than "belief in"
Belief is an activity of logos
Faith is about letting go of control,
and being in the moment.
Trusting that I am not alone
no matter what I feel
'cause mostly I feel alone—
Bereft.
Am I so insensitive to the numinous
that I don't experience its presence?
Or is it that there isn't a presence to be experienced?
"Like as a hart desireth water brooks
so longeth my soul for thee, O God."[34]

---

33 A reference to Process Theology.
34 Giovanni Pierluigi da Palestrina, *Sicuit Cervus,* (Like as a Hart), 1604.

Flying Free

Eyes opened slowly.
How long had they been closed?
Swamp home.
Redolent with miasma and verdancy
How long had she been here?
Wings, stiff from disuse
gingerly stretched, assessed.
Faint whiff of freshness.
Flashes a kestrel.
Gone.
Where?
Dare she follow?
Ephemeral images:
Fresh, clear air.
Sunlight reflected on moving water.
Barely remembered, or maybe only dreamed.
Dare she?
Leave?
Home?
Freshness…
Opportunity…
Test stroke, another, rising…
Home recedes
Sanctuary—refuge not lost,
rather, joined by new horizons.

War

Holy Father,
Sacred Mother,
God and goddess in unity.
Teach us the way of peace
so that our wars may end,
and all are held with respect.
Let us not use discord as a reason for shouting out
more loudly the rightness of our way.
May we listen with open hearts
and acknowledge our common humanity.
Let us look forward to the time
when we can sing with the psalmist:
"You have turned my mourning into dancing; you have taken off my
sackcloth and clothed me with joy, so that my soul may praise you and
not be silent.
O Lord, my God,
I will give thanks to you forever" (Ps 30:11-12 NRSVue).
May it be so.
Blessed be.

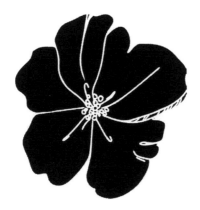

Free Will

Loving Father, Gracious Mother.
What does it mean to follow your will?
Is everything mapped out so that
I just follow the rut carved for me?
Or does life happen merely as cause and effect?
Are you an agent in the great web of being?
Am I like an insect caught in my part of the web,
awaiting my time to be devoured?
In faith, I affirm your presence, love, and grace.
In faith, I say I get a choice.
Perhaps a path may be planted in my soul
that will be revealed as the moment arises.
And I can choose whether to follow it.
So, choice and holy will abide.
I choose free will.

Let Spirit Work

What do I have to say?
All is vanity—
a whistling in the wind.
Yet, I listen.
Maybe this time
I'll feel the connection.
It has been said that trying harder
is not the way to go.
Relax and let Spirit do its work.
What work might that be?
Spirit, what do you wish to do with me?

Wu Wei

Holy Presence,
I turn to you in my need.
My life has become unmanageable.
My "to-dos" are myriad,
and multiply without ceasing.
My pulse races—
My body shakes—
I want to go to sleep to escape.
Holy Presence,
I turn to you in my need.
One thing is needful.
That I dwell in your heart
as you dwell in mine.
May *wu wei*[35] become my way.
And so, it is.
Blessed be.

35 The School of Life, "Taoist principle in Chinese.wu wei." https://www.
theschooloflife.com/article/wu-wei-doing-nothing/ (accessed 3/30/2022), "Doing
nothing, all is done."

Shoulds

Gracious Creator,
who camps among us.
The questions come.
What do I need today?
What should I do?
Yes, that word, should,
which "should" be expunged from our
contemplations.
But I need help to plan and prioritize,
and still be open to the
possibilities that arise.
"Lead me, O LORD, in your righteousness…
make your way straight before me" (Ps 5:8 NRSVue).

Listen to Your Heart

Sanctus Mysterium,
the One who holds me
in the palm of their hand.
Teach me to be in tune with Your heartbeat,
testing words with reason
just as reason must be
guided by heart.
And to listen even more deeply
for my soul's voice
whose wisdom outshines all others.
May it be so.
Dea/Deo Gratias.

Tuned

Loving Presence,
Who dwells within.
Thank You for this gift
which is of my very self.
Tuned to hear Your voice,
and dance to Your song.
May it ever be so.
Blessed be.

Doing Nothing, All Is Done

Holy Mystery,
Who loves me because I am.
Teach me this dynamic stillness
whereby, in doing nothing,
all is changed.
By following this path, glimpses of comprehension will appear.
I don't need to understand to walk this way.

Stick-to-itiveness

O my soul,
why are you so lacking in constancy?
Why do you flit from thing to thing
finishing almost nothing?
Yes, I know you get bored.
And there is always something new
that catches your fancy.
But this inability to stay on task
is troublesome—
at least as much a bother as
practicing stick-to-itiveness.
May I learn to balance the two disciplines—
doing and being.
May my doing arise from my being.
May it be so.

Lies

Depression lies.
How do these maggots get in my head?
Why do I believe them
instead of soaking up affirmations?
Why do I block the positive?
It's like my mind is full of bindweed.
Only extreme measures put a dent in it.
And it is never totally removed.
How then should I live?

This Day

Holy, holy, holy,
"This is the day that the LORD has made.
Let us rejoice and be glad in it" (Ps 118:24 NRSVue).
Except, I can't.
I bemoan my lot
while surrounded by a plethora of possibilities.
My mind goes blank
in the face of all these choices.
They feel like burdens,
weighing me down with "to-dos."
How rude to whine in the face of abundance.
Multiplicity devolves into boredom.
Please, save me from myself.
May I be set free from these "shoulds" and "to-dos."
May I trust your gentle prodding
so that the next step is mindfully taken.
Dea/Deo Gratias.

Holy Listening

Holy Presence,
Intimate Friend.
So, this is how it works.
Not writing in the sky
but whisperings in the heart
which find their way to
the head for expression.
I'm barely aware that this occurs.
But the evidence is in my hand
as I write these prayers—
as I seek to understand.

Hope

Holy Spirit
Blessed Presence
I present to you my hopes for
a vibrant practice
A vibrant life
fully expressing your gifts of "love, joy, peace, patience, kindness,
generosity, faithfulness, **23** gentleness, and self-control" (Gal 5:22-23
NRSVue).
And when I trip, or worse,
may I "look to you and be radiant" (Ps. 34:5a NRSVue).
Letting my failure fall away,
knowing that you love me,
because I am an expression of you.
May I love that divine spark, that *chispa*[36], within me,
and rest in peace.
Blessed be.

---

36 spark in Spanish.

Blue Heron

She came to me, a great blue heron.
"Climb on."
I scrambled on her back,
and off we flew.
"Where are we going?"
"We're going home."
"Is my death imminent?"
"No, you are going home to yourself."

Affirmations

Holy Spirit,
I can trust my heart.
I am light.
The Goddess and I are one.
I am love and loved.
May I be an open channel
tuned to your frequency.

Holy Light

Holy Light,
shining in the midst of confusion.
Let there be light created out of this abyss.
Let there be light to lead me on my way.
Let there be light shining within me,
that I might be a light-bearer this day.
And the Creator sees that it is good.
Dea/Deo Gratias.

Celebration

Dear Goddess within,
Mother of all that is.
A day of celebration and commitment
to embark on a quest.
One for seeking and receiving—
opening to insights,
plumbing the depths,
and re-learning to fly.
Thus, your light will glow more brightly
from my heart
exuding warmth, empathy, surprises, and joy.
And so, it is.
Blessed be.

True Nature

Loving Presence,
my true nature.
May I rest in you
as you live in me.
Letting our light shine
for the common good.
May it be so.

Journey

Lodestar for the wanderer,
Alpha and Omega of all our journeying.
I know not what lies ahead
yet trust that You go before me
Calling my name to help me with next steps.
As the path appears before me.

Longing

How I long for you, Most High.
"As a deer longs for flowing streams"… (Ps 42:1 NRSVue).
"…more than those who watch for the morning" (Ps 130:6 NRSVue).
But is this really a longing for myself?
What could it mean to long for myself?

Be Still

"Be still and know that I am God" (Ps. 46:10 NRSVue)!
How to be still when there's so much to do?
Clean the house, keep up with the finances,
water the garden, and the inside forest of plants...
Who has time to think about healthy meals?
And cooking them is beyond the realm of possibility.
"Be still" echoes in my mind.
In stillness
the panic falls away.
In stillness is peace.
It is time with the Belovèd who longs for time with me.
It is time with myself
since that is where the Belovèd abides.
But the many things—
be still. One thing is needful.
There will be time enough
for the many things.

Sparkle

May I sparkle as the living sacrament love has called into being.
May my every act arise from compassion.
May I add to the peace of the world all my days,
and turn to Spirit to guide my ways.
May my service be a reflection of my commitment to love.
In so doing, I will play my part in the sacred harmony
which resounds throughout the universe.
I make this covenant with all.
Blessed be.

Small Talk

Holy Mystery,
what shall we talk about today?
The strife in the world?
The birds welcoming spring
even though snow still spots the ground?
That "all is vanity" (Eccl 1:2b. NRSVue)
even though hope seeps in?
How then shall we live?
In grace and thanksgiving
with hearts as conduits of Your love.

SERVICE

Indwelling

Intimate Spirit,
may I dwell in the light of your countenance,
being illumined by your mercy and grace.
So that all I do
embodies and reflects your Love.
So mote it be.

Hineni

Holy Mystery.
Hineni! [37]
Your servant.
One.
Who opens to your leading,
providing sacred space to all.
Amen.

Open Heart

Merciful Mother, Gracious Father,
"Have mercy on me
According to Your steadfast love" (Ps 51:1a NRSVue).
According to Your abundant compassion
I open my heart to Your presence
that I might be a light-bearer in your service
Bringing comfort to all.

---

37   Hebrew for "Here I am."

Serve With Gladness

Great Spirit,
Intimate Friend.
May I
"Make a joyful noise to the LORD, all the earth.
² Serve the LORD with gladness;
come into his presence with singing.
Know that the Lord is God.
It is he who made us, and we are his;
we are his people and the sheep of his pasture" (Ps 100:1-3 NRSVue).
For I am yours.
You rest in me.
May I walk this day
acknowledging your ever-present grace.
Dea/Deo Gratias.

The Dream

Holy Mystery, Sacred One.
I bring to you this dream.
Planted long ago, and now ready to grow.
Teach me what fertilizer to use,
and how to prune what needs to be cut away.
Help me weather the dry spells,
and dance in the rain
so that sweet fruit will appear in the fullness of time.
May this harvest be nourishment for many,
including myself.
May it be so.
Blessed be.

Presence of Love

Holy Mystery,
who calls me to be
the presence of love in the world.
Since you dwell in my heart
and I in yours
Answering that call with my life
is my holy responsibility,
and an act of love.
Blessed be.

Sacrament

Holy Spirit,
who calls me into sacramental relationships.
Let me remember I am.
A vessel of Your love
to be poured out continually
as I open to Your ever-present grace.
Blessed be. May it be so.

Alchemist

Holy Mystery,
who infuses all there is.
Who has said, "See, I am making all things new" (Rev 21:5 NRSVue).
We are called to be alchemists in your service
To take whatever appears in our lives,
and use even dross to create blessing.
Dea/Deo Gratias.

Open Hearts

Our hearts open to the warmth of Your sun.
It melts the clouds of fear and sadness
Drives the depth of doubt away.
As it reaches every crevice,
I am able to reflect this light today.[38]
No matter how small.
As you breathe through me
may blessings abound,
and offerings of praise and thanks
become a constant stream from my heart.
Dea/Deo Gratias.

Gifts of Doing

Holy Mother, Sacred One.
Like Martha, I am busy with many things.[39]
Am I missing the one thing needful?
And that would be?
And who is going to clean up the mess?
Who does the laundry and dishes?
Who makes sure the "saints" are fed?
Humbly, I beseech thee
accept these gifts of doing.
May they be evidence of a servant's heart
You will not despise.

---

38 Henry Van Dyke, "Hymn to Joy," 1907, paraphrase by C. Coates.
39 (Luke 10:38-42 NRSVue).

PRESENCE

Awaken

You are always coming into my life, Belovèd,
and your light is forever illuminating my confusion.
Awaken me to your presence.
Give me eyes to see signs of hope,
ears to hear promises of grace and peace,
and a heart open to receive and channel your gifts of love.
May it be so.

Home

Welcome home.
Where is that? Where am I at home?
The problem is—I am not at home within myself.
I live surrounded by a cloud of judgmentalism.
I tiptoe around, so no one can hear or see me.
I am afraid of being discovered.
By whom? I don't know.
Where can I be at home?
It's a place in my mind.
A tidy cottage
Flowers surround it.
I can cook wholesome meals,
and sleep in sheets that are always cool.
(Unless it is winter, and I want warm sheets).
People come to visit,
and we share our hearts.
I pour tea.
They leave satisfied.
I am content.

Fountain

O my soul,
for what do you long?
"To know and be known by you, Belovèd."
I open my heart, and attune my ear to your voice.
May I become a fountain of compassion
Overflowing
for the benefit of all.

Bound by Love

Holy Mystery
I am yours
You are mine
Bound by love.
May I walk with You
all my days
a living sacrament:
visible sign of Your indwelling grace.
Light of light, I open my heart to You
that You might dwell there forever
as I will dwell in Yours.
Blessed be.

Alpha and Omega

Holy Mystery,
Alpha and Omega,
my source and my resting place.
Thank you for your care of me.
Lifting me up on eagles' wings
Sheltering me day and night.
May I walk humbly in Your sight
as you teach me the way of Your statutes.
Blessing, honor, glory, and power
You share with creation
Attending me all my days.
Dea/Deo Gratias.

Bread Baker God

Holy LORD[40], creator of all.
We are grateful for the system that makes life possible
Sun and harvest and hands and hearts, rain and rich soil.
We praise you as our bread of life.
Thank you for your action in our lives.
Through yeast and kneading and waiting and watching.
Shape our lives into full, fat loaves
that we may be nourishment where there is want,
be in our soul's every rising.[41]

---

40 Craig Phillips, Ph.D., 2021, In These Times, "The Loaf Keeper of All Creation,"
In These Tunes, 8/29/2021, https://craigphillips.co/2021/08/29/the-loaf-keeper-of-all-
creation/, accessed 8/16/2022). According to the Oxford English Dictionary, "lord" is
derived from the Old English word hláford, once hláfweard, which means "loaf-ward,"
that is the "keeper of the loaf." A lord, then, is the bread-keeper for the family. He was
the head of the household in relation to all who ate his bread.
41 Originally conceived in a workshop at Third Presbyterian Church, Rochester, NY,
facilitated by The Rev. Dr. Pat Youngdahl. Adapted by Catherine Coates.

Dona Nobis Pacem

Holy Spirit.
May I be a channel of your
presence this day.
A lantern through which Your
light shines.
Your light, with which my light co-mingles
Sparkling with Your love.
Dona nobis pacem.[42]
May it spring forth
throughout the earth.
Blessed be.

Only Love

Sanctus Mysterium.
I have spent years trying to figure out
a way to You.
Engaging my mind;
searching for answers.
But it turns out
I won't find You with my intellect.
Only love opens the door to You.

---

42 Grant us peace.

INTIMACY

Hearts as One

May our hearts beat as one, Most High,
rising from the depths where I cry.
Wholly, Holy, One,
You are my rock and my buckler.
With You is salvation and hope.
Even when the lions roar,
and I am embattled by grief.
To You will I turn
with each step I take,
trusting Your presence and love.
Blessed be.

Master Potter

"Just like the clay in the potter's hand, so are you in my hand, O house of Israel" (Jer. 18:6b. NRSVue).

Master Potter,
may I be pliable in Your hands
with a softened heart,
that the person within me emerge
as you see best.
[Now, wait a minute. I know where this is going.
Surrender! Let go and let God! Let God what? I always say].
"Hush, child. You haven't let me finish.
You are not in the hands of an angry god.
You are my hands in the world.
And like the scene from the movie *Ghost*,[43]
You are in my embrace as you turn the potter's wheel."

---

43 "Potter's Wheel Scene," Ghost, directed by Jerry Zucker, (1990; Hollywood, CA, Paramount Pictures). Before actor Patrick Swayze as Sam Wheat is murdered, he and the love of his life, Molly Jensen, as played by Demi Moore, embrace while she is making pottery at the potter's wheel. It is an incredible, sensual vision of passion and love.

Belovèd

Sanctus Mysterium
I don't know what to say.
Who are You?
"Your Belovèd.
Who calls you belovèd."
You touch my heart
with peacefulness and love.
Who are You?
"Your Belovèd.
One who loves you as you are,
dings and wounds and failures.
Who rejoices in your successes.
Who rejoices in you."
Who are you?
Wrapping Your arms around me—
accepting, comforting, sharing joy and sorrow—
intimacy.
We permeate each other like lovers.
Whither can I flee from You[44]
my Belovèd?
You are my soul's deepest longing:
to love and be loved.

---

44 Where can I go from your spirit? Or where can I flee from your presence? If I ascend to heaven, you are there; if I make my bed in Sheol, you are there (Ps 139:7-8 NRSVue).

Insemination

Holy Presence.
I will prepare a place for You
in my wilderness—
so that I might sup with You—
make love with You—
once sated, to rest in Your peace.
You plant in me Your seed.
It is mine to nurture and tend.
To labor.
So what was sown in darkness
blossoms into Love.
Together we share the joy of new creation—
with deep gratitude.
Blessed be.

Choices

Loving Presence.
within and without.
What would it be like to be enveloped by You?
I would be free of guilt.
Judgment would be no more.
I would have more courage
and less self-pity.
The inner critic would go on
permanent vacation.
I would make better choices about my health,
and let go of things that no longer serve me.
Your light would shine through me
so all could see Your glory.
Amen.

DEATH

My mother died suddenly when she was 58. As one can imagine, this was very traumatic. She was cremated and placed in a cardboard box. For some reason, my dad didn't acquire an urn. I was present when she was buried. On the box was written, "This is not a permanent container." I thought that was the best news I had heard since she died. We do not live in permanent containers.

Should I Stay or Should I Go?

Holy One,
Whose ways are mysterious.
I could use a little clarity in my life.
Should I stay or should I go?
Stay or go where?

On Death

Loving Receiver of Souls,
Divine Chatelaine.
Thank you for the life of my belovèd:
for the care and gentleness that comforted them;
for the prayers that uplifted them.
No key is needed to open heaven's door to them
for all are welcomed there.
And they will be met with open arms by those who have loved them.
Especially you, Most Holy.
Dea/Deo Gratias.

Terminal Disease

Terminal disease—a certain death sentence.
Not that any of us are exempt,
but there is a difference between
knowing that at some point we'll take that walk,
and knowing the hows, wheres, and probable whens—
it is too much to take in.
The mind boggles, the heart quakes,
the longing for a stay of execution is sharp.
How does one get in touch with the grace that is ever present?
Feelings of grief must come first.
And fury as the light slowly dims.
Peace and comfort may eventually pierce the terror
but not while it is so fresh
Time—I need time…

Resting in Your Arms

To Mystery watching over us.
"He who keeps you will not slumber…
will neither slumber nor sleep" (Ps. 121:3 NRSVue).
May my1 belovèd know Your presence
and rest in Your arms.
Letting go as they are able.
May we trust this process
and live into the grief.
Dea/Deo Gratias.

Letting Go

Divine Comforter.
Keeper of "your going out and your coming in" (Ps 121:8)
Let my belovèd feel your presence
Let them know that it is okay to let go.
Let me know that it is okay to let them go.
Life is precious.
That is why it is so hard to say goodbye.
Life is a gift—as is our passing into eternal life.
Dea/Deo Gratias.

Transition

Holy Mystery,
Eternal Comforter.
My belovèd is taking the path toward You.
May I come to see this transition as a blessing
while still immersed in grief.
Hold my belovèd by the hand to guide their way
back to family, friends, and especially their belovèd.
Dea/Deo Gratias.

Angel of Death

Angel of Death,
Help from God.
Who greets us at the door of transition.
I live in your presence continually.
The door may open at any time.
Grant me wisdom and vision
to prepare for that hour.
All the while embracing life
in its fullness.
Dea/Deo Gratias.

Miserere Mei

Holy Mystery,
Who embraces me in my grief.
Speaking tenderly.
Weeping empathetically.
Holding me in the palm of Your hand.
Miserere Mei, Dea[45]
And so, it is.

---

45 Have mercy on me, goddess.

Guide

Holy Presence
Guide for my days.
Much needs to be done.
So much, my grief is held at bay—
a cushion, perhaps, to soften the initial blow.
May my love be foremost
as I prepare for these final moments.
May Your wisdom guide me on my way.
Dea/Deo Gratias.

Weeping

Holy Mother of us all,
She who embraces each one.
Enfold me in Your arms this day.
So much has happened
I am exhausted and heart-broken by it all.
Our Mother weeps with us in our pain.
May her comfort and peace envelop all who grieve.
Dea/Deo Gratias.

Death's Door

"Death is not the extinguishing of the light; it is only putting out the lamp because the dawn has come," [46]

Holy Mystery,
Greeter at death's door.
When the time comes,
may my arms be open to Your embrace.
May I welcome the next life
as Your gift to me,
as this life has been a gift.
May my fear drop away,
that I may be infused with Your love, peace, and joy.
Blessed Be.
Dea/Deo Gratias.

---

46 Rabindranath Tagore, "Death," Brainyquote.com, https://www.brainyquote.com/quotes/rabindranath_tagore_386459.

For Janet

Who faced ALS on her own terms, and taught me what it means to die with dignity and without fear.

You're in a cave. There is very little light, and you have no sense of whence it arises. You remember light from earlier times, when there was warmth and laughter, growing and loving, and living fully. It seems a long time ago; it seems that you've been in this cave for a long time—too long. You keep moving through it, trying to find a source of the light. Then, ahead, a pinprick of light appears. You stumble toward it, hardly believing your eyes. You reach the opening, and before you is a place you've only dreamed about: verdant; butterflies and birdsong; a lake in the distance with a sailboat waiting at the shore. You walk slowly, taking it all in, but eventually you climb in the boat, knowing very well how to manage it. You set sail for the horizon, knowing you are going home. Blessed Be.

FINAL THOUGHTS

Breathe

Breathe.
May I be filled with Loving Kindness.
May I be Well.
May I be Open and Accepting.
May I be full of Gratitude.
Breathe.
Be.
Be Well.
Blessed be.
Be.
Breathe.
Intimate Spirit,
as Your light shines in me,
may my light shine
with compassion and peace.
Breathe.

Completeness

Holy Mystery,
losing myself in You
is not self-abnegation.
It is freedom to relax, and thus release
my true nature.
Which is always present
and has peeked out when it felt safe.
It's not about hating the self, the persona.
Rather, I am learning to fly free.
There isn't a goal of becoming better.
There is a journey towards completeness,
which never ends,
I am loved as I am.
I am loved into a more perfect union with Holy Mystery.

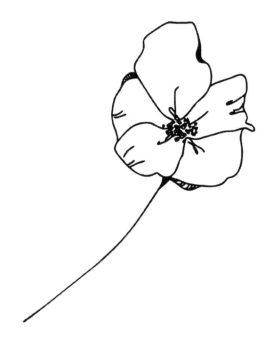

Life in Balance

Koyaanisqatsi,[47]
life out of balance
Moving too quickly
without being rooted in the earth.
Ikigai, a life of meaning,[48]
a life in balance,
deeply rooted
with the freedom to fly.
I will do what I love,
And bring my gifts to the world,
being compensated for what I do.
That all may be well with me.

Vessel

I have spent much of my life in the valley of the shadow.
I can now take this opportunity to revel in the dawning of light in
my life.
Holy arms are enfolding me.
I can trust them, even if/when there will be times the light seems dim.
Bask in the love that surrounds me, and is in me.
I am a vessel of holy light.
Let that light shine.
May it be so.
Blessed be.

---

47   *Koyaanisqatsi: Life Out of Balance.* directed by Godfrey Reggio, (1982, IRE
Production).
48   For further reading on *ikigai*: Erin Eatough, PhD., 2021, "What is *ikigai* and How
Can it Change my Life?" BetterUp.com, 5/7/2021, https://www.betterup.com/blog/
what-is-ikigai (Accessed 8/27/2022).

Let It Be a Dance[49]

"Whosoever knoweth the power of the dance, dwelleth in God. Without love, all worship is a burden, all dancing is a chore, all music is mere noise."

Holy Spirit,
Sacred One.
As Your light dances in our hearts,
may we learn the steps to dance with You in our lives.
Sometimes awkward with splats abounding.
Sometimes exuberant, wild with ecstasy, our feet barely touching the floor.
Sometimes exhausted, barely moving, like at the end of a dance marathon.
The waltz, the whirling dervish, the Virginia Reel, the jitterbug, the mashed potato—however the Spirit moves.
May I dance in Your arms this day,
remembering to let You lead.
Dea/Deo Gratias.
Hope is hearing the melody of the future; faith is dancing to it today[50].

---

49 Jalal ad-Din Muhammad Rumi, "Rumi's Dance," Art of Saudade.com, https://artofsaudade.com/2021/12/14/rumis-dance/, (Accessed 8/25/2022).
50 Ruben Alvez in Molly Fumia, ([2003], 2012 *Safe Passage: Words to Help the Grieving*, San Francisco: Conari Press imprint of Red Wheel/Weiser LLC.

Blessing of Holy Mystery

May the light of Holy Mystery shine
within you and through you.
May her healing spirit
fill your heart.
May his wisdom guide you.
May her love embrace you.
May you revel in their grace
which is ever present;
and,
may their peace bless you
all the days of your life.
Namaste,
Amen,
Amin,
Ashé,
A-Ho,
Om, shanti shanti **shanti**.
And so, it is.
Blessed be.

BIBLIOGRAPHY

Bain, James Leith Macbeth. "Brother James Air." 1915. Lyrics adapted by C. Coates.

da Palestrina Giovanni Pierluigi. *Sicuit Cervus.* (Like as a Hart).1604.
Denver, John. "Sunshine On My Shoulders." 1971. Lyrics by C. Coates.

Fumia, Molly. *Safe Passage: Words to Help the Grieving.* (2003), 2012. Conari Press imprint of Red Wheel/Weiser LLC.

Howe, Everett. "I Believe In the Sun, Part V: The Source." HumanistSeminarian. 2021. https://humanistseminarian.com/2021/04/04/i-believe-in-the-sun-part-v-the-source/.

Kempton, Sally. "Cutting Loose." Esquire Magazine. 1970.

L'Engle, Madeleine. "View." QuoteFancy,com. https://quotefancy.com/quote/999924/Madeleine-L-Engle-I-have-a-point-of-view-You-have-a-point-of-view-God-has-view.

Merrill, Nan C. *Psalms for Praying. An Invitation to Wholeness* (10th Anniversary ed.) (2007), 2016. London: 'Continuum Publishing, used by kind permission of Bloomsbury Publishing Plc.

New Revised Standard Version Updated Edition [Scripture quotations are from New Revised Standard Version Bible Updated Edition, copyright © (1989), 2022 National Council of the Churches of Christ in the United States of America. Used by permission. All rights reserved worldwide.]

Neyhart, Jennifer. "CS Lewis on Sehnsucht Longing and Desire in The Weight of Glory." 2014. https://www.jenniferneyhart.com/2014/10/c-s-lewis-on-sehnsucht-longing-and.html.

Phillips, Craig. In These Times. "The Loaf-Keeper of all Creation." 2021 https://craigphillips.co/2021/08/29/the-loaf-keeper-of-all-creation/.

Prudentius, Aurelius Clemens. *Divinum Mysterium,* circa 400 CE. Lyrics by C. Coates.

Rūmī, Jalāl al-Dīn Muhammad. Art of Saudade. "Rumi's Dance." https://artofsaudade.com/2021/12/14/rumis-dance/.

—. The Poetry Exchange,co,uk."The Guest House." https://www.thepoetryexchange.co.uk/the-guest-house-by-rumi.

—. Goodreads. "Your heart knows…" https://www.goodreads.com/quotes/9941552-.

Shakespeare, William. Hamlet. 3.1.58.

Tallis, Thomas. "God Grant with Grace." 1567. Lyrics by C. Coates.

Van Dyke, Henry. "Hymn to Joy."1907. paraphrase by C. Coates.

Wolfelt, Alan D. *Grief One Day at a Time.* Quoting Roos, Francis Ellis. 2016. Ft. Collins, CO: Companion Press.

Zucker, Jerry, director. *Ghost.* Paramount Pictures 1990. 2:08:00.

FOR FURTHER READING

Beyer, Catherine. "The Difference Between Magic and Magick." Learnreligions.com.2019. https://www.learnreligions.com/magic-and-magick-95856.

Eatough, Erin. "What is *ikigai* and how can it change my life?" BetterUp. com. 2021. https://www.betterup.com/blog/what-is-ikigai.

Mukherjee, Sushmita. "Ganesha. The 'Disabled God.'" On-Seeing.com. 2022. https://www.on-seeing.com/home/2022/9/4/ganesh-the-disabled-god.

Tagore, Rabindranath. "Death." Brainy Quotes. https://www.brainy-quote.com/quotes/rabindranath_tagore_386459.

Tarbox, Elizabeth. "All is Dukkha." 2015. http://www.cascadeuu.org/wp-content/uploads/2015/09/Wisdom-from-our-Sources-July-3.pdf.

Vallicella, Bill. "Creation ex Nihilo or ex Deo," Maverick Philosopher. 2016 https://maverickphilosopher.typepad.com/maverick_philosopher/2016/10/creation-ex-nihilo-or-ex-deo.html.

"Wu Wei – Doing Nothing." The School of Life. nd. https://www.theschooloflife.com/article/wu-wei-doing-nothing/.

About the Author

Having studied at One Spirit Learning Alliance, **The Rev. Catherine Coates** is an ordained interspiritual minister, and trained spiritual counselor. After a varied career in office work, the food industry, and data management, she has turned her writing into something she can share with others. Spiritual counseling is another way she offers her gifts of compassion, empathy, and intuition.

You can contact Catherine through her website, **catherinecoates.com** and on facebook at **www.facebook.com/catherine.coates.5.**

www.floweroflifepress.com